THE JOKIEST

JOKING **KNOCK-KNOCK** JOKE

BOOK EVER WRITTEN ... NO JOKE!

LOOKING FOR MORE JOKES TO IMPRESS
YOUR FRIENDS AND BUILD YOUR
ULTIMATE JOKEMASTER COLLECTION?

YOU'LL LOVE THE JOKIEST JOKING JOKE
BOOK EVER WRITTEN . . . NO JOKE!

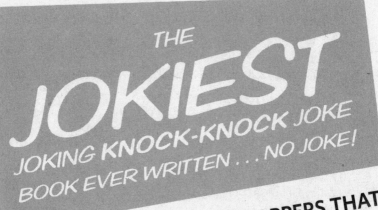

THE JOKIEST
JOKING KNOCK-KNOCK JOKE BOOK EVER WRITTEN . . . NO JOKE!

1,001 BRAND-NEW KNEE-SLAPPERS THAT WILL KEEP YOU LAUGHING OUT LOUD

Jokes by Brian Boone

Illustrations by Amanda Brack

CASTLE POINT BOOKS

NEW YORK

The Library of Congress Cataloging-in-Publication Data is available upon
request.

ISBN 978-1-250-16346-2 (trade paperback)
ISBN 978-1-250-16347-9 (ebook)

Our books may be purchased in bulk for promotional, educational, or
business use. Please contact your local bookseller or the Macmillan
Corporate and Premium Sales Department at 1-800-221-7945, extension
5442, or by email at MacmillanSpecialMarkets@macmillan.com.

First Edition: February 2018

10 9 8 7 6 5 4 3 2 1

Knock knock! WHO'S THERE?

My favorite kid. MY FAVORITE KID WHO?

You know who, it's you!

CONTENTS

Knock knock! *Who's there?*
The world's greatest. *The world's greatest who?*
The world's greatest and most varied, complete, and jam-packed knock-knock joke book of all time!

Welcome to The Jokiest Joking Knock-Knock Joke Book Ever Written . . . No Joke! *We put together more than 1,000 knock-knock jokes about every subject under the sun, along with some hilarious illustrations! Inside you'll find knock-knock jokes revolving around hundreds of names (is yours in here?), famous people, fictional characters, animals, food, places, jobs, and everyday objects. You'll even find some that are too random and silly to be believed.*

Here's one to get you started:

Knock knock! *Who's there?*

Orange. *Orange who?*

Orange you glad you picked up this book?

Knock knock! *Who's there?*
Renee. *Renee who?*
Renee marathon today!

Knock knock! *Who's there?*
Daisy. *Daisy who?*
Daisy plays, but at nights he goes to sleep.

Knock knock! *Who's there?*

Aida. *Aida who?*

Aida lot of sweets, and now I have a tummy ache.

Knock knock! *Who's there?*

Alexia. *Alexia who?*

Alexia again to open this door!

Knock knock! *Who's there?*

Arlette. *Arlette who?*

Arlette a fly in, sorry.

Knock knock! *Who's there?*

Athena. *Athena who?*

Athena flying saucer!

Knock knock! *Who's there?*

Carmen. *Carmen who?*

Carmen get it!

Knock knock! *Who's there?*

Celeste. *Celeste who?*

Celeste time I'm going to tell you!

Knock knock! *Who's there?*

Danielle. *Danielle who?*

Danielle, I heard you the first time!

Knock knock! *Who's there?*

Irene. *Irene who?*

Irene and Irene, but still no one answers the door!

Knock knock! *Who's there?*

Harmony. *Harmony who?*

Harmony times do I have to tell you?

Knock knock! *Who's there?*

Wilma. *Wilma who?*

Wilma frog turn into a prince?

Knock knock! *Who's there?*

Julie. *Julie who?*

Julie your door open, but I knocked anyway.

Knock knock! *Who's there?*

Bree. *Bree who?*

Bree a good neighbor, and let me in.

Knock knock! *Who's there?*

Frida. *Frida who?*

Frida the dark, open up!

Knock knock! *Who's there?*

Candace. *Candace who?*

Candace be love I'm feeling right now?

Knock knock! *Who's there?*

Isabella. *Isabella who?*

Isabella out of order?

Knock knock! *Who's there?*

Izzy. *Izzy who?*

Izzy come, Izzy go.

Knock knock! *Who's there?*

Olivia. *Olivia who?*

Olivia me alone!

Knock knock! *Who's there?*

Guinevere. *Guinevere who?*

Guinevere going to get together?

Knock knock! *Who's there?*

Lauren. *Lauren who?*

Lauren order.

Knock knock! *Who's there?*

Lois. *Lois who?*

Lois man on the totem pole, I'm afraid.

Knock knock! *Who's there?*

Mandy. *Mandy who?*

Mandy lifeboats, the ship's sinking!

Knock knock! *Who's there?*

Nona. *Nona who?*

Nona your business!

Knock knock! *Who's there?*

Nadia. *Nadia who?*

Nadia head if ya understand what I'm saying, okay?

Knock knock! *Who's there?*

Esther. *Esther who?*

Esther anybody else here for the party yet?

Knock knock! *Who's there?*

Hannah. *Hannah who?*

Hannah me some of those oranges, I'm starving!

Knock knock! *Who's there?*

Maya. *Maya who?*

Maya hand is killing me from knocking all day!

Knock knock! *Who's there?*

Anna. *Anna who?*

Anna chance you wanna go out later?

Knock knock! *Who's there?*

Enid. *Enid who?*

If Enid anything, I'm here.

Knock knock! *Who's there?*

Ida. *Ida who?*

Ida called first.

Knock knock! *Who's there?*

Tamara. *Tamara who?*

Tamara we'll see!

Knock Knock! Who's there?

Joanne. Joanne who?

Joanne tell!

Knock knock! *Who's there?*

Denise. *Denise who?*

Denise are in the middle of your legs.

Knock knock! *Who's there?*

Wanda. *Wanda who?*

Wanda where I left my keys!

Knock knock! *Who's there?*

Lisa. *Lisa who?*

Lisa you could do is let me in.

Knock knock! *Who's there?*

May. *May who?*

May I come in already?

Knock knock! *Who's there?*

Gwen. *Gwen who?*

Gwen do you think you want to come out?

Knock knock! *Who's there?*

Tori. *Tori who?*

Tori I bothered you.

Knock knock! *Who's there?*

Norma Lee. *Norma Lee who?*

Norma Lee I'd ring the doorbell.

Knock knock! *Who's there?*

Halle. *Halle who?*

Hallelujah, I'm here to sing!

Knock knock! *Who's there?*

Eve. *Eve who?*

Evening!

Knock knock! *Who's there?*

Liz. *Liz who?*

Liz roll! We're going to be late.

Knock knock! *Who's there?*

Lydia. *Lydia who?*

Lydia teapot looks a bit loose. Shall I fix it?

Knock knock! *Who's there?*

Isabel. *Isabel who?*

Isabel really necessary when you have such a great door knocker?

Knock knock! *Who's there?*

Anya. *Anya who?*

Anya best behavior please!

Knock knock! *Who's there?*

Annie. *Annie who?*

Annie body home?

Knock knock! *Who's there?*

Allie. *Allie who?*

Allie want for Christmas is you!

Knock knock! *Who's there?*

Meg. *Meg who?*

Meg up your mind!

Knock knock! *Who's there?*

Leda. *Leda who?*

Leda of the pack. *Vroom-vroom!*

Knock knock! *Who's there?*

Sarah. *Sarah who?*

Sarah doctor in the house? These jokes are making me sick.

Knock knock! *Who's there?*
Bella. *Bella who?*
Bella button full of lint!

Knock knock! *Who's there?*
Della. *Della who?*
I want to Della 'nother knock-knock joke, if you don't mind.

Knock knock! *Who's there?*
Lena. *Lena who?*
Lena bit closer and I'll tell you.

Knock knock! *Who's there?*
Alison. *Alison who?*
Alison to this new song!

Knock knock! *Who's there?*
Darby. *Darby who?*
Darby pirates about!

Knock knock! *Who's there?*

Holly. *Holly who?*

Holly-days are here already!

Knock knock! *Who's there?*

Shirley. *Shirley who?*

Shirley you know who!

Knock knock! *Who's there?*

Sadie. *Sadie who?*

Sadie magic words and I'll tell you.

Knock knock! *Who's there?*

Olga. *Olga who?*

Olga home if you aren't nice.

Knock knock! *Who's there?*

Wendy. *Wendy who?*

Wendy today, sunny tomorrow.

Knock knock! *Who's there?*

Debbie. *Debbie who?*

Debbie stung me! Or maybe it was a wasp.

Knock knock! *Who's there?*

Abby. *Abby who?*

Abby birthday to you!

Knock knock! *Who's there?*

Anna. *Anna who?*

Anna one, Anna two . . .

Knock knock! *Who's there?*

Ivana. *Ivana who?*

Ivana you to let me in!

Knock knock! *Who's there?*

Clara. *Clara who?*

Clara space, I'm coming in for dinner!

Knock knock! *Who's there?*

Susan. *Susan who?*

Susan socks keep your feet warm.

Knock knock! *Who's there?*

Colleen. *Colleen who?*

Colleen up this mess out here!

Knock knock! *Who's there?*

Mara. *Mara who?*

Mara-Mara on the wall, who's the fairest of them all?

Knock knock! *Who's there?*

Wendy. *Wendy who?*

Wendy last time you brushed your teeth?!

Knock knock! *Who's there?*

Amanda. *Amanda who?*

Amanda fix the toilet!

Knock knock! *Who's there?*

Sabrina. *Sabrina who?*

Sabrina long time since I've seen you!

Knock knock! *Who's there?*

Sasha. *Sasha who?*

Sasha lot of questions!

Knock knock! *Who's there?*

Sloane. *Sloane who?*

Sloanely out here.

Knock knock! *Who's there?*

Bonnie. *Bonnie who?*

Bonnie long time since last we spoke!

Knock knock! *Who's there?*

Bailey. *Bailey who?*

I know we Bailey know each other, but can we hang out?

Knock knock! *Who's there?*

Tish. *Tish who?*

Yes, thank you—I need to blow my nose.

Knock knock! *Who's there?*

Alma. *Alma who?*

Alma treasure is buried on an island, argh!

Knock knock! *Who's there?*

Alda. *Alda who?*

Alda time you knew who it was!

Knock knock! *Who's there?*

Yvonne. *Yvonne who?*

Yvonne to be alone?

Knock knock! *Who's there?*

Linda. *Linda who?*

Linda hand, I can't move this piano by myself!

Knock knock! *Who's there?*

Rita. *Rita who?*

Rita book—you might learn something!

Knock knock! *Who's there?*

Amy. *Amy who?*

Amy 'fraid I've forgotten!

Knock knock! *Who's there?*

Mia. *Mia who?*

Mia and my shadow.

Knock knock! *Who's there?*

Mischa. *Mischa who?*

I Mischa lots!

Knock knock! *Who's there?*

Mae. *Mae who?*

Mae-be I'll say, and Mae-be I won't.

Knock knock! *Who's there?*

Marie. *Marie who?*

Marie me—I love you!

Knock knock! *Who's there?*

Phyllis. *Phyllis who?*

Phyllis cup up with water please, I'm so thirsty!

Knock knock! *Who's there?*

Claire. *Claire who?*

Claire the way, I'm coming through!

Knock knock! *Who's there?*

Roxanne. *Roxanne who?*

Roxanne coral are my favorite things about the beach!

Knock knock! *Who's there?*

Violet. *Violet who?*

Violet your cat in and out while you're away, will you bring me back a souvenir?

Knock knock! *Who's there?*
Eliza. *Eliza who?*
Eliza lot, so don't trust him.

Knock knock! *Who's there?*
Kim. *Kim who?*
Kim too late to the party.

Knock knock! *Who's there?*
Stephanie. *Stephanie who?*
Stephanie gas, we're going to be late!

Knock knock! *Who's there?*
Henrietta. *Henrietta who?*
Henrietta worm that was in his apple! Gross!

Knock knock! *Who's there?*

Vicky. *Vicky who?*

Vicky to a good health is a balanced diet.

Knock knock! *Who's there?*

Darlene. *Darlene who?*

Be a Darlene and open the door for me?

Knock knock! *Who's there?*

Alice. *Alice who?*

Alice fair in love and war!

Knock knock! *Who's there?*

Dee. *Dee who?*

Dee cake is in dee oven!

Knock knock! *Who's there?*

Penny. *Penny who?*

Penny for your thoughts?

Knock knock! *Who's there?*

Sonya. *Sonya who?*

What's Sonya to-do list for today?

Knock knock! *Who's there?*

Dawn. *Dawn who?*

Dawn mess around here, or I'll take off!

Knock knock! *Who's there?*

Taylor. *Taylor who?*

Taylor little brother to pick up his toys so I don't step on them.

Knock knock! *Who's there?*

Jess. *Jess who?*

Jess me!

Knock knock! *Who's there?*

Erin. *Erin who?*

I have to run a quick Erin, but I'll be right back!

Knock knock. *Who's there?*

Avery. *Avery who?*

Avery nice person is knocking on the door, you should come take a look!

Knock knock! *Who's there?*

Iris. *Iris who?*

Iris you were here!

Knock knock! *Who's there?*

Cameron. *Cameron who?*

Turn your Cameron and take a picture of me!

Knock knock! *Who's there?*

Lee. *Lee who?*

I'm lone Lee without you!

Knock knock! *Who's there?*

Frances. *Frances who?*

Frances next to Spain, you know.

Knock knock! *Who's there?*

Harriet. *Harriet who?*

Harriet up, and open the door!

Knock knock! *Who's there?*

Yardley. *Yardley who?*

Yardley know you, but can I come in?

Knock knock! *Who's there?*

Wanda. *Wanda who?*

Wanda hang out for a bit?

Knock knock! *Who's there?*

Daria. *Daria who?*

Daria getting tired of these silly jokes yet?

Knock knock! *Who's there?*

Bette. *Bette who?*

Bette you can't guess!

Knock knock! *Who's there?*

Dana. *Dana who?*

Dana talk to me like that!

Knock knock! *Who's there?*

Samantha. *Samantha who?*

Samantha time you're nice, but not right now!

Knock knock! *Who's there?*

Elsie. *Elsie who?*

Maybe Elsie you around some time?

Knock knock! *Who's there?*

Ivy. *Ivy who?*

Ivy good mind to keep going and going and going . . .

Knock knock! *Who's there?*

Viola. *Viola who?*

Viola sudden you pretend not to know me?

Knock knock! *Who's there?*

Maura. *Maura who?*

Maura knock-knock jokes on the way!

Knock knock! *Who's there?*

Stella. *Stella who?*

Stella more jokes to each other!

Knock knock! *Who's there?*

Val. *Val who?*

Val, how are you doing?

Knock knock! *Who's there?*

Sharon. *Sharon who?*

Sharon share alike!

Knock knock! *Who's there?*

Joan. *Joan who?*

Joan you remember me?

Knock knock! *Who's there?*
Brighton. *Brighton who?*
Brighton early, I said I'd be here!

Knock knock! *Who's there?*
Cynthia. *Cynthia who?*
Cynthia been so good, I'm taking you out to dinner!

Knock knock! *Who's there?*
Annette. *Annette who?*
Annette from you and a pole from me, and we're sure to catch a fish.

Knock knock! *Who's there?*
Justice. *Justice who?*
Justice I thought—you don't remember me!

Knock knock! *Who's there?*
Rhona. *Rhona who?*
Rhona bike around all day and I'm so tired!

Knock knock! *Who's there?*

Alex. *Alex who?*

Hey, Alex the questions around here!

Knock knock! *Who's there?*

Ruth. *Ruth who?*

Ruth of the matter is that I'm glad to see you!

Knock knock! *Who's there?*

Leia. *Leia who?*

Leia down and go to sleep.

Knock knock! *Who's there?*

Candace. *Candace who?*

Candace be the last knock-knock joke?

Knock knock! *Who's there?*
Ralph. *Ralph who?*
Ralph! Ralph! I'm a dog!

Knock knock! *Who's there?*
Raoul. *Raoul who?*
Raoul with the punches.

Knock knock! *Who's there?*

Ray. *Ray who?*

Ray-member me always!

Knock knock! *Who's there?*

Reid. *Reid who?*

Reid-turning to your house, like I said I would.

Knock knock! *Who's there?*

Bowen. *Bowen who?*

Bowen arrow is all you need for archery.

Knock knock! *Who's there?*

Quentin. *Quentin who?*

Quentin my thirst drinking out of your garden hose!

Knock knock! *Who's there?*

Quincy. *Quincy who?*

Quincy me right now if you like!

Knock knock! *Who's there?*

Toby. *Toby who?*

Toby or not Toby, that is the question.

Knock knock! *Who's there?*

Buck. *Buck who?*

Buck, buck, I'm a chicken!

Knock knock! *Who's there?*

Duane. *Duane who?*

Duane the tub, I'm dwowning!

Knock knock! *Who's there?*

Emerson. *Emerson who?*

Emerson nice shoes you've got on.

Knock knock! *Who's there?*

Emmett. *Emmett who?*

Emmett your service!

Knock knock! *Who's there?*

Hugo. *Hugo who?*

Hugo your way, and I'll go mine.

Knock knock! *Who's there?*

Willie. *Willie who?*

Willie . . . or won't he?

Knock knock! *Who's there?*

Fletcher. *Fletcher who?*

Fletcher self have a little fun!

Knock knock! *Who's there?*

Omar. *Omar who?*

Omar goodness gracious, I knocked on the wrong door!

Knock knock! *Who's there?*

Kenny. *Kenny who?*

Kenny stay for dinner if he calls his mom?

Knock knock! *Who's there?*

Keith. *Keith who?*

Keith me, you fool!

Knock knock! *Who's there?*

Luke. *Luke who?*

Luke out—here comes another knock-knock joke.

Knock knock! *Who's there?*

Oliver. *Oliver who?*

Oliver tomatoes are getting snatched.

Knock knock! *Who's there?*

Wayne. *Wayne who?*

The Wayne is really coming down out here!

Knock knock! *Who's there?*

Neville. *Neville who?*

Neville you mind that, can I come in?

Knock knock! *Who's there?*

Harry. *Harry who?*

Harry up and let me in!

Knock knock! *Who's there?*

Bryan. *Bryan who?*

Just Bryan stop me from knocking!

Knock knock! *Who's there?*

Jim. *Jim who?*

Jim mind if I come in?

Knock knock! *Who's there?*

Alex. *Alex who?*

Alex-plain when you open the door!

Knock knock! *Who's there?*

Al. *Al who?*

Al give you some candy if you let me in.

Knock knock! *Who's there?*

Scott. *Scott who?*

Scott nothing to do with you!

Knock knock! *Who's there?*

Hugh. *Hugh who?*

Hugh do you think it is?

Knock knock! *Who's there?*

Amos. *Amos who?*

Amos-quito just bit me!

Knock knock! *Who's there?*

Andy. *Andy who?*

Andy bit me again!

Knock knock! *Who's there?*

Ewan. *Ewan who?*

It's just me.

Knock knock! *Who's there?*

Kent. *Kent who?*

Kent you tell who this is?

Knock knock! *Who's there?*

Ben. *Ben who?*

Ben knocking all morning!

Knock knock! *Who's there?*

Adair. *Adair who?*

Adair once, but now I'm bald.

Knock knock! *Who's there?*

Philip. *Philip who?*

Philip my bag with treats this Halloween!

Knock knock! *Who's there?*

Frank. *Frank who?*

You're welcome!

Knock knock! *Who's there?*

Meyer. *Meyer who?*

Meyer nosy!

Knock knock! *Who's there?*

Henry. *Henry who?*

Henry body gonna let me in?

Knock knock! *Who's there?*

Fred. *Fred who?*

Fred chicken for dinner tonight!

Knock knock! *Who's there?*

Barry. *Barry who?*

Barry sorry for what I did!

Knock knock! *Who's there?*

Juan. *Juan who?*

Juan more minute and I'm leaving!

Knock knock! *Who's there?*

Sam. *Sam who?*

Sam person who knocked before.

Knock knock! *Who's there?*

Adolf. *Adolf who?*

Adolf ball just whacked me in the head!

Knock knock! *Who's there?*

Mikey. *Mikey who?*

Mikey doesn't fit in the keyhole!

Knock knock! *Who's there?*

Alvy. *Alvy who?*

Alvy right here if you need me.

Knock knock! *Who's there?*

Theodore. *Theodore who?*

Theodore was locked, so I knocked.

Knock knock! *Who's there?*

Stefan. *Stefan who?*

Stefan the bug quick before it bites me!

Knock knock! *Who's there?*

Isaiah. *Isaiah who?*

Isaiah nothing until you open this door!

Knock knock! *Who's there?*

Howie. *Howie who?*

I'm fine. How are you?

Knock knock! *Who's there?*

Ike. *Ike who?*

Ike haven't got a clue.

Knock knock! *Who's there?*

Mister. *Mister who?*

Mister last bus home. Can I stay here?

Knock knock! *Who's there?*

Ivor. *Ivor who?*

Ivor sore hand from knocking!

Knock knock! *Who's there?*

Simon. *Simon who?*

Simon the other side of the door. Open up and see!

Knock knock! *Who's there?*

Stu. *Stu who?*

Stu early to go to bed.

Knock knock! *Who's there?*

Earl. *Earl who?*

Earl be glad when it's summer!

Knock knock! *Who's there?*

Raymond. *Raymond who?*

Raymond me to go to the store—we're out of milk.

Knock knock! *Who's there?*

Les. *Les who?*

Les cut the chit-chat and open this door, huh?

Knock knock! *Who's there?*

Brett. *Brett who?*

Brett you don't know who this is!

Knock knock! *Who's there?*

Archie. *Archie who?*

Archie ever gonna open up?

Knock knock! *Who's there?*

Carson. *Carson who?*

Carson the freeway go so fast.

Knock knock! *Who's there?*

Doug. *Doug who?*

Doug deep in my bag and still couldn't find my keys!

Knock knock! *Who's there?*

Alden. *Alden who?*

Alden with dinner? Then come outside!

Knock knock! *Who's there?*
Harold. *Harold who?*
Harold do you think I am?

Knock knock! *Who's there?*
Lucas. *Lucas who?*
Lucas in the eye and tell us you don't want to read any more knock-knock jokes, and we'll stop.

Knock knock! *Who's there?*
Mano. *Mano who?*
Mano few words, that's why I knock.

Knock knock! *Who's there?*
Gary. *Gary who?*
Gary me inside, I'm so tired!

Knock knock! *Who's there?*

Moe. *Moe who?*

Moe knock-knock jokes then?

Knock knock. *Who's there?*

Ernest. *Ernest who?*

Ernest is full of chicken eggs.

Knock knock! *Who's there?*

Walter. *Walter who?*

Walter you doing up so early?

Knock knock! *Who's there?*

Conner. *Conner who?*

Conner brother come out and play?

Knock knock! *Who's there?*

Collin. *Collin who?*

Just Collin to tell you another knock-knock joke.

Knock knock! *Who's there?*

Benjamin. *Benjamin who?*

Benjamin to the music all day, dude.

Knock knock! *Who's there?*

Manny. *Manny who?*

Manny people keep asking me that!

Knock knock! *Who's there?*

Seymour. *Seymour who?*

Seymour if you look out the window.

Knock knock! *Who's there?*

Hans. *Hans who?*

Hans off!

Knock knock! *Who's there?*

Filmore. *Filmore who?*

Filmore confident and open the door.

Knock knock! *Who's there?*

Aloysius. *Aloysius who?*

Aloysius that you'd let me in!

Knock knock! *Who's there?*

Ethan. *Ethan who?*

Ethan though you don't like my jokes, can you let me in?

Knock knock! *Who's there?*

Tad. *Tad who?*

Tad's how you treat me after all these years?

Knock knock! *Who's there?*

Hubie. *Hubie who?*

Hubie a pal and bring me a cookie?

Knock knock! *Who's there?*

Max. *Max who?*

Max no difference to me.

Knock knock! *Who's there?*

Hal. *Hal who?*

Hal-lo to you, too!

Knock knock! *Who's there?*

Paul. *Paul who?*

Paul up a chair and I'll tell you!

Knock knock! *Who's there?*

Carl. *Carl who?*

Carl get you there faster than a bike.

Knock knock! *Who's there?*

Horatio. *Horatio who?*

Horatio to the end of the street! Go!

Knock knock! *Who's there?*

Adam. *Adam who?*

Adam my way, I'm coming through!

Knock knock! *Who's there?*

Rufus. *Rufus who?*

Rufus covered in snow, so let me in before it slides onto me!

Knock knock! *Who's there?*

Tyrone. *Tyrone who?*

Tyrone shoelaces!

Knock knock! *Who's there?*

Saul. *Saul who?*

It's Saul over now.

Knock knock! *Who's there?*

Willis. *Willis who?*

Willis ever get old, telling each other these knock-knock jokes?

Knock knock! *Who's there?*

Olaf. *Olaf who?*

Olaf these years, I've wondered where you lived!

Knock knock! *Who's there?*

Warren. *Warren who?*

Warren the world have you been?!

Knock knock! *Who's there?*

Otto. *Otto who?*

Otto know. Who are you?

Knock knock! *Who's there?*

Chad. *Chad who?*

Chad to make your acquaintance!

Knock knock! *Who's there?*

Ken. *Ken who?*

Ken you tell me some good knock-knock jokes?

Knock knock! *Who's there?*

Jimmy. *Jimmy who?*

If you Jimmy a key, I can let myself in.

Knock knock! *Who's there?*

Will. *Will who?*

Will you listen to another knock-knock joke?

Knock knock! *Who's there?*

Eddie. *Eddie who?*

Eddie body home?

Knock knock! *Who's there?*

Gino. *Gino who?*

Gino, these jokes are pretty fun!

Knock knock! *Who's there?*

Otto. *Otto who?*

You really Otto open the door.

Knock knock! *Who's there?*

Russell. *Russell who?*

Let's Russell up some grub!

Knock knock! *Who's there?*
Orson. *Orson who?*
Stop Orson around!

Knock knock! *Who's there?*
Giovanni. *Giovanni who?*
Giovanni come outside or what?

Knock knock! *Who's there?*
Wes Q. *Wes Q. who?*
Help, help, Wes Q. me!

Knock knock! *Who's there?*
Phineas. *Phineas who?*
Phineas thing happened to me today.

Knock knock! *Who's there?*
Hewlett. *Hewlett who?*
Hewlett the dogs out?

Knock knock! *Who's there?*

Edward B. *Edward B. who?*

Edward B. very nice to see you.

Knock knock! *Who's there?*

Anson. *Anson who?*

Anson my pants!

Knock knock! *Who's there?*

Upton. *Upton who?*

Upton no good, I see!

Knock knock! *Who's there?*

Levi. *Levi who?*

Levi the door unlocked next time!

Knock knock! *Who's there?*

Watson. *Watson who?*

Watson TV tonight?

Knock knock! *Who's there?*

Darren. *Darren who?*

Darren you to open the door.

Knock knock! *Who's there?*

Oswald. *Oswald who?*

Uh-oh, Oswald my bubblegum!

Knock knock! *Who's there?*

Rudy. *Rudy who?*

Rudy you to keep me waiting!

Knock knock! *Who's there?*

Walt. *Walt who?*

Walt! Who goes there?

Knock knock! *Who's there?*

Michael. *Michael who?*

Michael you on the phone before I come over next time.

Knock knock! *Who's there?*

Randy. *Randy who?*

I Randy whole way over here!

Knock knock! *Who's there?*

Uriah. *Uriah who?*

Keep Uriah the ball, slugger!

Knock knock! *Who's there?*

Richard. *Richard who?*

Richard poor, I'll like you just the same.

Knock knock! *Who's there?*

Jeff. *Jeff who?*

Jeff you wait!

Knock knock! *Who's there?*

Reggie. *Reggie who?*

Reggie to go yet?

Knock knock! *Who's there?*

Cain. *Cain who?*

Cain you come out and play catch?

Knock knock! *Who's there?*

Trevor. *Trevor who?*

Trevor you mind about that!

Knock knock! *Who's there?*

Jonah. *Jonah who?*

Jonah who else lives around here?

Knock knock! *Who's there?*

Vinnie. *Vinnie who?*

Vinnie you gonna let me in?

Knock knock! *Who's there?*

Stanton. *Stanton who?*

Stanton here answering questions is no fun!

Knock knock! *Who's there?*

Arlo. *Arlo who?*

Arlo can you go?

Knock knock! *Who's there?*

Woody. *Woody who?*

Woody like to hear another knock-knock joke?

3
WILD KINGDOM

Knock knock! *Who's there?*

Udder. *Udder who?*

Would you like to hear an udder knock-knock joke?

Knock knock! *Who's there?*

Achilles. *Achilles who?*

Achilles mosquitos if they don't quit biting me!

Knock knock! *Who's there?*

Mike Howell. *Mike Howell who?*

Mike Howell give you lots of milk!

Knock knock! *Who's there?*

Arnold. *Arnold who?*

Arnold dog can't learn new tricks!

Knock knock! *Who's there?*

Conch. *Conch who?*

Conch you come outside for a while?

Knock knock! *Who's there?*

Lionel. *Lionel who?*

Lionel bite you if you get too close at the zoo!

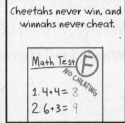

Knock knock! *Who's there?*

Distinct. *Distinct who?*

Distinct of de skunk out here is de worst!

Knock knock! *Who's there?*

Gibbon. *Gibbon who?*

Why are you Gibbon me such a hard time?

Knock knock! *Who's there?*

Polly Warner. *Polly Warner who?*

Polly Warner cracker?

Knock knock! *Who's there?*

Whale. *Whale who?*

Whale, whale, whale, what have we here?

Knock knock! *Who's there?*

Sham. *Sham who?*

Sham-u, the killer whale!

Knock knock! *Who's there?*

Kelp. *Kelp who?*

Kelp me get a gift for my mom.

Knock knock! *Who's there?*

Fido. *Fido who?*

Fido away, will you miss me?

Knock knock! *Who's there?*

Rabbit. *Rabbit who?*

Rabbit up and let's go!

Knock knock! *Who's there?*

Quacker. *Quacker who?*

Quacker 'nother bad joke and I'm outta here!

Knock knock! *Who's there?*

Flea. *Flea who?*

Flea blind mice, flea blind mice, see how they run, see how they run . . .

Knock knock! *Who's there?*

Oink-oink. *Oink-oink who?*

Are you a pig or an owl?

Knock knock! *Who's there?*

Ocelot. *Ocelot who?*

Ocelot of questions, don't you?

Knock knock! *Who's there?*

Dog. *Dog who?*

Dog-gone it, open the door!

Knock knock! *Who's there?*

Cows go. *Cows go who?*

No, cows go moo.

Knock knock! *Who's there?*

Amoeba. *Amoeba who?*

Amoeba silly, but I really like knock-knock jokes!

Knock knock! *Who's there?*

Dino. *Dino who?*

Dino-mite!

Knock knock! *Who's there?*

Spider. *Spider who?*

Spider what everyone says, I like you!

Knock knock! *Who's there?*

Newt. *Newt who?*

Newt to this neighborhood, can you show me around?

Knock knock! *Who's there?*

Viper. *Viper who?*

Viper nose, it's running!

Knock knock! *Who's there?*

Honeybee. *Honeybee who?*

Honeybee a dear, and go get me a soda.

Knock knock! *Who's there?*

Geese. *Geese who?*

Geese what I'm going to do if you don't open the door!

Knock knock! *Who's there?*

Tick. *Tick who?*

Is tock there? It's time we got back together!

Knock knock! *Who's there?*

Baby owl. *Baby owl who?*

Baby owl see you around sometime?

Knock knock! *Who's there?*

Panther. *Panther who?*

Panther what you wear on your legths.

Knock knock! *Who's there?*

Robin. *Robin who?*

Robin your house!

Knock knock! *Who's there?*

Meow. *Meow who?*

Take meow to the ball game . . .

Knock knock! *Who's there?*

Feline. *Feline who?*

Feline fine, thanks for asking! You?

Knock knock! *Who's there?*

Moose. *Moose who?*

Moose you always be so suspicious?

Knock knock! *Who's there?*

Gnats. *Gnats who?*

Gnats not funny!

Knock knock! *Who's there?*

Weevil. *Weevil who?*

Weevil stay just a minute, promise!

Knock knock! *Who's there?*

Beehive. *Beehive who?*

Beehive yourself!

Knock knock! *Who's there?*

Stork. *Stork who?*

Stork up on food—storm's a comin'!

Knock knock! *Who's there?*

Ostrich. *Ostrich who?*

Ostrich my arms up to the sky!

Knock knock! *Who's there?*

Toucan. *Toucan who?*

Well, toucan play that game!

Knock knock! *Who's there?*

Giraffe. *Giraffe who?*

Giraffe anything to eat in there?

Knock knock! *Who's there?*

Heron. *Heron who?*

Heron any knock-knock jokes you like yet?

Knock knock! *Who's there?*

Bee. *Bee who?*

Bee yourself!

Knock knock! *Who's there?*

Badger. *Badger who?*

I'll badger no more if you let me in!

Knock knock! *Who's there?*

Elephant. *Elephant who?*

You forgot to feed the elephant!

Knock knock! *Who's there?*

Bat. *Bat who?*

Bat you'll let me in soon.

Knock knock! *Who's there?*

Fur. *Fur who?*

Waiting fur you to open the door.

Knock knock! *Who's there?*
Chimp. *Chimp who?*
I think it's pronounced shampoo.

Knock knock! *Who's there?*
Pooch. *Pooch who?*
Pooch your arms around me, baby!

Knock knock! *Who's there?*
Claws. *Claws who?*
Claws the door behind you.

Knock knock! *Who's there?*
Possum. *Possum who?*
Possum food to me, I'm hungry!

Knock knock! *Who's there?*

A herd. *A herd who?*

A herd you were home so I came right over.

Knock knock! *Who's there?*

Beaver. *Beaver who?*

Beaver quiet, and no one will hear us!

Knock knock! *Who's there?*

Kanga. *Kanga who?*

No, kangaroo!

Knock knock! *Who's there?*

Hee-haw. *Hee-haw who?*

Well, are you a donkey or an owl?

Knock knock! *Who's there?*

Koala. *Koala who?*

Koala the cops, I've been robbed!

Knock knock! *Who's there?*

Collie. *Collie who?*

Collie-flower is good for you.

Knock knock! *Who's there?*

Mustang. *Mustang who?*

Mustang up the phone and answer the door!

Knock knock! *Who's there?*

Safari. *Safari who?*

Safari so good.

Knock knock! *Who's there?*

Anteater. *Anteater who?*

Anteater dinner, but Uncle wasn't hungry.

Knock knock! *Who's there?*

Weasel. *Weasel who?*

Weasel while you work . . .

Knock knock! *Who's there?*

Otter. *Otter who?*

You otter apologize to me!

Knock knock! *Who's there?*

Howl. *Howl who?*

Howl you know . . . unless you open the door?

Knock knock! *Who's there?*

I lecture. *I lecture who?*

I lecture dog out of the yard, sorry!

Knock knock! *Who's there?*

Wood ant. *Wood ant who?*

Don't be afraid, I wood ant hurt a fly!

Knock knock! *Who's there?*

Cat. *Cat who?*

Cat you think of a better joke than that?

Knock knock! *Who's there?*

Cattle. *Cattle who?*

Cattle purr if you pet her.

Knock knock! *Who's there?*

Goose. *Goose who?*

Goose see a doctor for that cough!

Knock knock! *Who's there?*

Rhino. *Rhino who?*

Rhino every single knock-knock joke!

4
CULTURE VULTURES

Knock knock! *Who's there?*

Elmo. *Elmo who?*

You don't know who Elmo is?

Knock knock! *Who's there?*

Merilee. *Merilee who?*

Merilee we roll along, roll along, roll along . . .

Knock knock! *Who's there?*

Joanna. *Joanna who?*

Joanna build a snowman?

Knock knock! *Who's there?*

Bashful. *Bashful who?*

I can't say—I'm too embarrassed!

Knock knock! *Who's there?*

Thor. *Thor who?*

Thor-ry, wrong house!

Knock knock! *Who's there?*

Dora. *Dora who?*

Dora my way, or I'd come on in with Map and Swiper.

Knock knock! *Who's there?*

Art. *Art who?*

Art-who-D-2. Beep-boop!

Knock knock! *Who's there?*

Dallas. *Dallas who?*

Dallas in Wonderland!

Knock knock! *Who's there?*

Alito. *Alito who?*

Alito of the pack.

Knock knock! *Who's there?*

Diarrhea. *Diarrhea who?*

Diarrhea wimpy kid.

Knock knock! *Who's there?*

Grinch. *Grinch who?*

Grinch who stole Christmas!

Knock knock! *Who's there?*

Siri. *Siri who?*

Siri, wrong house!

Knock knock! *Who's there?*

Yah. *Yah who?*

No, I use Google.

Knock knock! *Who's there?*

Fantastic Four. *Fantastic Four who?*

Fantastic Four you to let us in already!

Knock knock! *Who's there?*

Jacqueline. *Jacqueline who?*

Jacqueline Hyde.

Knock knock! *Who's there?*

Eeyore. *Eeyore who?*

Eeyore not letting me in, and that makes me sad!

Knock knock! *Who's there?*

Milhouse. *Milhouse who?*

Milhouse is empty, can I come hang out with you for a while?

Knock knock! *Who's there?*

Popeye. *Popeye who?*

Popeye wanna talk to you, you in there with Ma?

Knock knock! *Who's there?*

Tintin. *Tintin who?*

Tintin happen to leave the door unlocked, I guess.

Knock knock! *Who's there?*

Shrek. *Shrek who?*

You Shrek me to stand out here all day and wait for you?

Knock knock! *Who's there?*

Mickey Mouse. *Mickey Mouse who?*

Mickey Mouse not be the right one, because I can't seem to unlock the door!

Knock knock! *Who's there?*

Romeo. *Romeo who?*

Romeo-nly me and Juliet out here!

Knock knock! *Who's there?*

Sherlock Holmes. *Sherlock Holmes who?*

Sherlock Holmes up, or somebody could break in.

Knock knock! *Who's there?*

Tigger. *Tigger who?*

Tigger treat!

Knock knock! *Who's there?*

Snow. *Snow who?*

There's snow place like home!

Knock knock! *Who's there?*

Only. *Only who?*

Only you can prevent forest fires!

Knock knock! *Who's there?*

Oz. *Oz who?*

Oz just about to tell you if you'd give me a second.

Knock knock! *Who's there?*

Narnia. *Narnia who?*

Narnia business.

Knock knock! *Who's there?*

Pink Panther. *Pink Panther who?*

Pink Panther all I have to wear, I better do some laundry!

Knock knock! *Who's there?*

Juicy. *Juicy who?*

Juicy that new movie trailer?

Knock knock! *Who's there?*

Sombrero. *Sombrero who?*

Sombrero-ver the rainbow . . .

Knock knock! *Who's there?*

Rupert. *Rupert who?*

Rupert your left foot in, Rupert your left foot out . . .

Knock knock! *Who's there?*

Ivan. *Ivan who?*

Ivan working on the railroad . . .

Knock knock! *Who's there?*

Captain Jack. *Captain Jack who?*

Captain Jack-ed your stuff. He is a pirate, after all.

Knock knock! *Who's there?*

Kermit. *Kermit who?*

Grab Kermit and a ball, and let's play catch!

Knock knock! *Who's there?*
Deduct. *Deduct who?*
Donald Deduct, quack-quack!

Knock knock! *Who's there?*
Sloane. *Sloane who?*
Sloane Ranger. Hi-ho, Silver!

Knock knock! *Who's there?*
Yachts. *Yachts who?*
Eh, yachts up, Doc?

Knock knock! *Who's there?*

Pooh. *Pooh who?*

Don't cry, I'm a friendly bear.

Knock knock! *Who's there?*

Moana. *Moana who?*

Moana come in for a while?

Knock knock! *Who's there?*

Belle. *Belle who?*

No, there's no need for ballyhoo, it's just me.

Knock knock! *Who's there?*

Mater. *Mater who?*

See you Mater, alligator!

Knock knock! *Who's there?*

Chicken Little. *Chicken Little who?*

The sky is falling!

Knock knock! *Who's there?*

Nemo. *Nemo who?*

Nemo knock-knock jokes? I've got plenty!

Knock knock! *Who's there?*

Mr. Incredible. *Mr. Incredible who?*

Mr., it's incredible you haven't let me in yet!

Knock knock! *Who's there?*

Jughead. *Jughead who?*

Jughead-ed out real soon!

Knock knock! *Who's there?*

Josie. *Josie who?*

Just Josie, no Pussycats.

Knock knock! *Who's there?*

Bond. *Bond who?*

Bond to succeed if you keep trying!

Knock knock! *Who's there?*

Smurfette. *Smurfette who?*

Smurfette all the smurfberries!

Knock knock! *Who's there?*

Fozzie. *Fozzie who?*

Fozzie last time, these are supposed to be funny! Wocka-wocka-wocka!

Knock knock! *Who's there?*

Gumby. *Gumby who?*

Gumby banned at school, so you better not bring any!

Knock knock! *Who's there?*

Hello Kitty. *Hello Kitty who?*

Hello Kitty, do you want some tuna?

Knock knock! *Who's there?*

Dory. *Dory who?*

Hi, I'm Dory. Want to hear a knock-knock joke?

Knock knock!

Who's there?

Richie Rich.

Richie Rich who?

Richie Rich you could at least say hi.

Knock knock!

Who's there?

Road Runner.

Road Runner who?

Beep-beep!

Knock knock!

Who's there?

Chip 'n' Dale.

Chip 'n' Dale who?

Chip, 'n', Dale cover the rest.

Knock knock!

Who's there?

Batman.

Batman who?

Just Batman. I work alone.

Knock knock!

Who's there?

Remy.

Remy who?

Remy come in there and make you some dinner!

Knock knock!

Who's there?

Stitch.

Stitch who?

Stitch you hear I like you?

5
REAL PEOPLE

Knock knock! *Who's there?*

Disney. *Disney who?*

I'm Disney from riding all those rides!

Knock knock! *Who's there?*

Abbott. *Abbott who?*

Abbott time you opened that door!

Knock knock!

Who's there?

Soldier.

Soldier who?

Soldier bike yet?

Knock knock!

Who's there?

Butcher.

Butcher who?

Butcher money where your mouth is.

Knock knock!

Who's there?

Mayan.

Mayan who?

Mayan the right neighborhood or not?

Knock knock!

Who's there?

Amish.

Amish who?

How sweet, Amish you too!

Knock knock!

Who's there?

Police.

Police who?

Police open the door.

Knock knock!

Who's there?

Police.

Police who?

What do you mean, "who"? We're the police. Open up!

Knock knock!

Who's there?

Deluxe.

Deluxe who?

Deluxe-smith. I'm here to fix de lock.

Knock knock!

Who's there?

IBM.

IBM who?

IBM. Who be you?

Knock knock!

Who's there?

Sis.

Sis who?

Sis any way to treat family?

Knock knock!

Who's there?

Farmer.

Farmer who?

Farmer distance, your house looks much larger.

Knock knock!

Who's there?

Midas.

Midas who?

Midas well open the door because I'm not leaving!

Knock knock!

Who's there?

Cousin.

Cousin who?

Cousin-stead of opening the door, you're making me stand out here!

Knock knock! *Who's there?*

Usher. *Usher who?*

Usher wish you would let me in!

Knock knock! *Who's there?*

Waiter. *Waiter who?*

Waiter minute while I tie my shoelace.

Knock knock! *Who's there?*

Countess. *Countess who?*

Does this countess a funny joke?

Knock knock!

Who's there?

Rockefeller.

Rockefeller who?

Rockefeller in his cradle, and he'll go right to sleep.

Knock knock!

Who's there?

Chauffeur.

Chauffeur who?

Chauffeur, I'm doing great, thanks!

Knock knock!

Who's there?

Jester.

Jester who?

Jester minute, hold on!

Knock knock!

Who's there?

Czar.

Czar who?

Czar a doctor in the house?

Knock knock!

Who's there?

The IRS.

The IRS who?

The IRS. And we are taking your house.

Knock knock!

Who's there?

Anne Boleyn.

Anne Boleyn who?

Anne Boleyn alley, go for a strike!

Knock knock! *Who's there?*

Burglar. *Burglar who?*

Burglars don't knock!

Knock knock! *Who's there?*

Stalin. *Stalin who?*

Stalin for time!

Knock knock! *Who's there?*

Huge liar. *Huge liar who?*

It's me, the Queen of England, honest!

Knock knock! *Who's there?*

Cher. *Cher who?*

Cher-lock Holmes!

Knock knock! *Who's there?*

Major. *Major who?*

Ha-ha, major ask!

Knock knock! *Who's there?*

Zookeeper. *Zookeeper who?*

Zookeeper away from me!

Knock knock! *Who's there?*

Kaley Cuoco. *Kaley Cuoco who?*

Kaley Cuoco to the park with me, so maybe you will?

Knock knock! *Who's there?*

Ben Stiller. *Ben Stiller who?*

Ben Stiller 'round? I'd like to say hi.

Knock knock! *Who's there?*

John Cena. *John Cena who?*

John Cena spider out here, and he got so scared he ran away!

Knock knock! *Who's there?*

Pharrell. *Pharrell who?*

Pharrell this knocking I'm doing, you don't seem to be coming to the door!

Knock knock! *Who's there?*

Scissor. *Scissor who?*

Scissor and Cleopatra!

Knock knock! *Who's there?*

Nick Jonas. *Nick Jonas who?*

Nick Jonas a cool new song he wrote!

Knock knock! *Who's there?*

Alka. *Alka who?*

Alka-pone, stick 'em up!

Knock knock! *Who's there?*

Pastor. *Pastor who?*

Pastor potatoes, I'm hungry.

Knock knock! *Who's there?*

G.I. *G.I. who?*

G.I. don't know!

Knock knock! *Who's there?*

Godson. *Godson who?*

I've godson good news and some bad news . . .

Knock knock! *Who's there?*
Stepfather. *Stepfather who?*
One stepfather and I'll be in!

Knock knock! *Who's there?*
Ringo. *Ringo who?*
Ringo round the collar.

Knock knock! *Who's there?*
Emma Watson. *Emma Watson who?*
Emma Watson 'nother piece of pie!

Knock knock! *Who's there?*

Nick Cannon. *Nick Cannon who?*

Nick Cannon stand you!

Knock knock! *Who's there?*

Imagine Dragons. *Imagine Dragons who?*

Imagine Dragons are in your house, so let me in to help!

Knock knock! *Who's there?*

Miley Cyrus. *Miley Cyrus who?*

Miley Cyrus at the mall together, and she's mad we didn't invite her.

Knock knock! *Who's there?*

Chris Pratt. *Chris Pratt who?*

Chris Pratt's all folks!

Knock knock! *Who's there?*

Alicia Keys. *Alicia Keys who?*

Alicia Keys still in there? She can't find 'em anywhere!

Knock knock! *Who's there?*

Daisy Ridley. *Daisy Ridley who?*

Daisy Ridley me this!

Knock knock!

Who's there?

Jennifer Lawrence.

Jennifer Lawrence who?

Jennifer Lawrence her house. Do you own your own house?

Knock knock!

Who's there?

Adele.

Adele who?

Helloooo . . .

Knock knock! *Who's there?*

Shoes. *Shoes who?*

Shoes me to come in there, and not anybody else!

Knock knock! *Who's there?*

Stopper. *Stopper who?*

Stopper, she just ran away with your newspaper!

Knock, knock! *Who's there?*

Accordion. *Accordion who?*

Accordion to the weather forecaster, it's going to rain tomorrow.

Knock knock! *Who's there?*

Statue. *Statue who?*

Statue? This is me.

Knock knock! *Who's there?*

Aisle. *Aisle who?*

Aisle see you around!

Knock knock! *Who's there?*

Jewel. *Jewel who?*

Jewel be sorry!

Knock knock! *Who's there?*

Freighter. *Freighter who?*

Freighter snakes? I know I am!

Knock knock! *Who's there?*

Adopt. *Adopt who?*

Adopt my pencil on the ground and it rolled away.

Knock knock! *Who's there?*

Thistle. *Thistle who?*

Thistle make you laugh!

Knock knock! *Who's there?*

Diesel. *Diesel who?*

Diesel man, he played one . . .

Knock knock! *Who's there?*
Swatter. *Swatter who?*
Swatter you doing later?

Knock knock! *Who's there?*
Iota. *Iota who?*
Iota leave!

Knock knock! *Who's there?*
York hat. *York hat who?*
York hat kept me up all night caterwauling!

Knock knock! *Who's there?*
Hair. *Hair who?*
Hair today, gone tomorrow!

Knock knock! *Who's there?*
Issue. *Issue who?*
Issue crazy? It's me!

Knock knock! *Who's there?*

Heart. *Heart who?*

Heart you glad to see me?

Knock knock! *Who's there?*

Knee. *Knee who?*

Knee-d you ask?

Knock knock! *Who's there?*

Icon. *Icon who?*

Icon tell you a different knock-knock joke if you like.

Knock knock! *Who's there?*

Diploma. *Diploma who?*

Diploma is here to fix de sink!

Knock knock! *Who's there?*

Fiddle. *Fiddle who?*

Fiddle make you happy, I guess I'll tell you.

Knock knock! *Who's there?*

Razor. *Razor who?*

Razor hands in the air like you just don't care!

Knock knock! *Who's there?*

Train. *Train who?*

Someone needs to train you to answer the door when people knock!

Knock knock! *Who's there?*

Mustache. *Mustache who?*

Please let me in, I mustache you an important question!

Knock knock! *Who's there?*

Bingo. *Bingo who?*

Bingo-ing to come see you for ages!

Knock knock! *Who's there?*

Chess. *Chess who?*

Me!

Knock knock! *Who's there?*

Tennis. *Tennis who?*

Tennis too many dogs for this small house!

Knock knock! *Who's there?*

Tide. *Tide who?*

Tide of these knock-knock jokes yet?

Knock knock! *Who's there?*

Ice. *Ice who?*

Ice to see you, too.

Knock knock! *Who's there?*

Eyes. *Eyes who?*

Eyes better come in before it gets too dark.

Knock knock! *Who's there?*

Rain. *Rain who?*

Rain, dear, like the ones that pull Santa's sleigh!

Knock knock! *Who's there?*

Weed. *Weed who?*

Weed better leave soon.

Knock knock! *Who's there?*

Ear. *Ear who?*

Ear you are, at long last!

Knock knock! *Who's there?*

Cargo. *Cargo who?*

Cargo "beep-beep!"

Knock knock! *Who's there?*

Radio. *Radio who?*

Radio not, here I come!

Knock knock! *Who's there?*

Dumbbell. *Dumbbell who?*

Dumbbell doesn't work so I had to knock!

Knock knock! *Who's there?*

Window. *Window who?*

Window you think we'll get tired of these knock-knock jokes?

Knock knock! *Who's there?*

Nose. *Nose who?*

I nose a lot more knock-knock jokes, if you're interested in hearing them.

Knock knock! *Who's there?*

Sonata. *Sonata who?*

Sonata big deal.

Knock knock! *Who's there?*

Comet. *Comet who?*

Comet a crime, and you'll go to prison.

Knock knock! *Who's there?*

Clothesline. *Clothesline who?*

Clothesline all over the floor are going to end up wrinkled.

Knock knock! *Who's there?*

Detail. *Detail who?*

Detail of de cat is on de end.

Knock knock! *Who's there?*

Atlas. *Atlas who?*

Atlas, you're home!

Knock knock! *Who's there?*

Stopwatch. *Stopwatch who?*

Stopwatch you're doing and open up!

Knock knock! *Who's there?*

Botany. *Botany who?*

Botany good books lately?

Knock knock! *Who's there?*

Dishwasher. *Dishwasher who?*

Dishwasher way I spoke before I got my dentures.

Knock knock! *Who's there?*

Acid. *Acid who?*

Acid down and be quiet!

Knock knock! *Who's there?*

Thermos. *Thermos who?*

Thermos be a better knock-knock joke than this one!

Knock knock! *Who's there?*

Cotton. *Cotton who?*

Cotton a trap. Help me get out!

Knock knock! *Who's there?*

Dots. *Dots who?*

Dots for me to know, and you to find out!

Knock knock! *Who's there?*

Ooze. *Ooze who?*

Ooze been telling you all these terrible knock-knock jokes?

Knock knock! *Who's there?*

Wooden shoe. *Wooden shoe who?*

Wooden shoe like to be my neighbor?

Knock knock! *Who's there?*

Bug spray. *Bug spray who?*

Bug spray that spiders won't eat them!

Knock knock! *Who's there?*

Saber. *Saber who?*

Saber, she's drowning!

Knock knock! *Who's there?*

Disguise. *Disguise who?*

Disguise de limit!

Knock knock! *Who's there?*

Wheel. *Wheel who?*

Wheel stop telling these jokes when we're good and ready!

Knock knock! *Who's there?*
Cadillac. *Cadillac who?*
Cadillac mad if you step on his tail.

Knock knock! *Who's there?*
Auto. *Auto who?*
Auto know, but I forgot.

Knock knock! *Who's there?*
Snow. *Snow who?*
This is snow time for questions, open up. It's snowing!

Knock knock! *Who's there?*
Dozen. *Dozen who?*
Dozen anybody wanna come out and play?

Knock knock! *Who's there?*

Hatch. *Hatch who?*

Have you got a cold or something?

Knock knock! *Who's there?*

Tire. *Tire who?*

Tire shoelaces or you'll trip and fall!

Knock knock! *Who's there?*

Nuisance. *Nuisance who?*

What's nuisance the last time I saw you?

Knock knock! *Who's there?*

Husk. *Husk who?*

Bless you!

Knock knock! *Who's there?*

Ore. *Ore who?*

Ore else!

Knock knock! *Who's there?*
Brick. *Brick who?*
Brick or treat!

Knock knock! *Who's there?*
Gunpowder. *Gunpowder who?*
Gunpowder my nose.

Knock knock! *Who's there?*
Stick. *Stick who?*
Stick around.

Knock knock! *Who's there?*
Armor. *Armor who?*
Armor friends in there?

Knock knock! *Who's there?*

Chest. *Chest who?*

Chest got back from vacation!

Knock knock! *Who's there?*

Arrow. *Arrow who?*

Arrow on the side of caution.

Knock knock! *Who's there?*

Oak. *Oak who?*

Oak out below!

Knock knock! *Who's there?*

Wool. *Wool who?*

Wool you let me in?

Knock knock! *Who's there?*
A boat. *A boat who?*
A boat time I got here.

Knock knock! *Who's there?*
Kimono. *Kimono who?*
Kimono my house sometime!

Knock knock! *Who's there?*
Zipper. *Zipper who?*
Zipper-dee-doo-dah!

Knock knock! *Who's there?*
Canoe. *Canoe who?*
Canoe *please* get off my foot?

Knock knock! *Who's there?*

Lavender. *Lavender who?*

Lavender world laughs with you.

Knock knock! *Who's there?*

Cologne. *Cologne who?*

Cologne Ranger!

Knock knock! *Who's there?*

Dew. *Dew who?*

Dew something about your room, it's a mess!

Knock knock!

Who's there?

Tree.

Tree who?

Tree more days until vacation!

Knock knock! *Who's there?*
Peas. *Peas who?*
Peas come outside.

Knock knock! *Who's there?*
Candy. *Candy who?*
Candy cow jump over the moon?

Knock knock! *Who's there?*

Foreign. *Foreign who?*

Foreign 20 blackbirds baked in a pie . . .

Knock knock! *Who's there?*

Papaya. *Papaya who?*

Papaya the Sailor Man.

Knock knock! *Who's there?*

Kumquat. *Kumquat who?*

Kumquat may, I'll always be your friend!

Knock knock! *Who's there?*

Pasta. *Pasta who?*

Pasta la vista, baby!

Knock knock! *Who's there?*

Icing. *Icing who?*

Icing really loud! LA-LA-LA-LAAAAAA!

Knock knock! *Who's there?*

Omelet. *Omelet who?*

Omelet smarter than I look!

Knock knock! *Who's there?*

Sultan. *Sultan who?*

Sultan pepper.

Knock knock! *Who's there?*

Anita. *Anita who?*

Anita borrow a cup of sugar.

Knock knock! *Who's there?*

Sturdy. *Sturdy who?*

Sturdy pot before it burns!

Knock knock! *Who's there?*

Annapolis. *Annapolis who?*

Annapolis what I eat each day to keep the doctor away!

Knock knock! *Who's there?*

Pasta. *Pasta who?*

Pasta pizza while it's still hot.

Knock knock! *Who's there?*

Tina. *Tina who?*

Tina fish sandwich!

Knock knock! *Who's there?*

Apricot. *Apricot who?*

Apricot my keys!

Knock knock! *Who's there?*

C.I.A. *C.I.A. who?*

C.I.A. the whole cake.

Knock knock! *Who's there?*

Ice cream soda. *Ice cream soda who?*

Ice cream soda whole world will know how silly I am!

Knock knock! *Who's there?*

Arthur. *Arthur who?*

Arthur any cookies left?

Knock knock! *Who's there?*

Distressing. *Distressing who?*

Distressing has too much vinegar!

Knock knock! *Who's there?*

Ketchup. *Ketchup who?*

Ketchup with you soon!

Knock knock! *Who's there?*

Artichokes. *Artichokes who?*

Artichokes when he eats too fast!

Knock knock! *Who's there?*

Boysen. *Boysen who?*

Boysen ivy!

Knock knock! *Who's there?*

Carrot. *Carrot who?*

Don't you carrot all about me?

Knock knock! *Who's there?*

Muffin. *Muffin who?*

Muffin the matter with me!

Knock knock! *Who's there?*

Turnip. *Turnip who?*

Turnip the heat, it's cold out here.

Knock knock! *Who's there?*

Water. *Water who?*

Water you waiting for?

Knock knock! *Who's there?*

Orange. *Orange who?*

Orange you going to let me in?

Knock knock! *Who's there?*

Brew. *Brew who?*

Hey, don't cry!

Knock knock! *Who's there?*

Seed. *Seed who?*

Seed what I did there?

Knock knock! *Who's there?*

Apple. *Apple who?*

Apple on the door but it won't budge!

Knock knock! *Who's there?*

Bacon. *Bacon who?*

Bacon you a cake for your birthday!

Knock knock! *Who's there?*

Fajita. *Fajita who?*

Fajita 'nother bite I'll burst.

Knock knock! *Who's there?*

Cod. *Cod who?*

Cod you please open up, it's so cold out here!

Knock knock! *Who's there?*

Shellfish. *Shellfish who?*

Don't be so shellfish.

Knock knock! *Who's there?*

Pear. *Pear who?*

Pear-jury is a serious offense!

Knock knock! *Who's there?*

Flounder. *Flounder who?*

We flounder guilty on all charges!

Knock knock! *Who's there?*

Catsup. *Catsup who?*

Catsup a tree and he can't get down!

Knock knock! *Who's there?*

Crab. *Crab who?*

Crab me before you leave, okay?

Knock knock! *Who's there?*

Honeydew. *Honeydew who?*

Honeydew you want to hear another knock-knock joke?

Knock knock! *Who's there?*

Kiwi. *Kiwi who?*

Kiwi go to the park and play right now?

Knock knock! *Who's there?*

Beef. *Beef who?*

Beef-ore I get cold, you better let me in.

Knock knock! *Who's there?*

Broccoli. *Broccoli who?*

Broccoli doesn't have a last name, you fool!

Knock knock! *Who's there?*

Cereal. *Cereal who?*

Cereal pleasure to meet you!

Knock knock! *Who's there?*

Weiner. *Weiner who?*

Weiner you going to let me in?

Knock knock! *Who's there?*

Gum. *Gum who?*

Gum on, let me in already!

Knock knock! *Who's there?*

Avocado. *Avocado who?*

Avocado cold, I'm afraid. *Sniff-sniff.*

Knock knock! *Who's there?*

Lime. *Lime who?*

Lime leaving if you don't open this door soon!

Knock knock! *Who's there?*

Stew. *Stew who?*

Stew you want me to make you lunch?

Knock knock! *Who's there?*

Cracker. *Cracker who?*

Cracker eggs too early and you won't be able to make breakfast!

Knock knock! *Who's there?*

Wok. *Wok who?*

I wok all the way over here and you won't even let me in?!

Knock knock! *Who's there?*

Cheese. *Cheese who?*

For cheese a jolly good fellow, for cheese a jolly good fellow . . .

Knock knock! *Who's there?*

Pizza. *Pizza who?*

I'm going to give you a pizza my mind!

Knock knock! *Who's there?*

Pesto. *Pesto who?*

I hate to make a pesto myself, but I'm going to keep knocking until you open the door!

Knock knock! *Who's there?*

Gluten. *Gluten who?*

You're a gluten for punishment, listening to all these knock-knock jokes!

Knock knock! *Who's there?*

Chicken. *Chicken who?*

Chicken to see if you still live here!

Knock knock! *Who's there?*

Samoa. *Samoa who?*

Samoa these cookies I'm selling?

Knock knock! *Who's there?*

Mustard. *Mustard who?*

Mustard be Thanksgiving if I'm here!

Knock knock! *Who's there?*

Egg roll. *Egg roll who?*

Egg roll off the table and it cracked.

Knock knock! *Who's there?*

Mint. *Mint who?*

Mint to tell you I was coming over.

Knock knock! *Who's there?*

Pecan. *Pecan who?*

Pecan somebody your own size!

Knock knock! *Who's there?*

Java. *Java who?*

Java lot to learn about manners!

Knock knock! *Who's there?*

Figs. *Figs who?*

Figs your doorbell!

Knock knock! *Who's there?*

Juicy. *Juicy who?*

Juicy what I just saw?!

Knock knock! *Who's there?*

Hominy. *Hominy who?*

Hominy times are we going to do this?

Knock knock! *Who's there?*

Yeast. *Yeast who?*

Yeast you could do is come to the door and say hello!

Knock knock! *Who's there?*

Peace. *Peace who?*

Peace porridge hot, peace porridge cold . . .

Knock knock! *Who's there?*

Pete. *Pete who?*

Pete-za delivery!

Knock knock! *Who's there?*

Howell. *Howell who?*

Howell you have your pizza, plain or with extra cheese?

Knock knock! *Who's there?*

Hammond. *Hammond who?*

Hammond eggs for breakfast again?

Knock knock! *Who's there?*

Nettie. *Nettie who?*

Nettie as a fruitcake!

Knock knock! *Who's there?*

Quiche. *Quiche who?*

Can I have a hug and a quiche?

Knock knock! *Who's there?*

Nacho cheese. *Nacho cheese who?*

Nacho cheese? Then give it back!

Knock knock! *Who's there?*

Hummus. *Hummus who?*

Hummus a tune if you don't know the words.

Knock knock! *Who's there?*

Fennel. *Fennel who?*

Fennel start when you let me in!

Knock knock! *Who's there?*

Pumpkin. *Pumpkin who?*

Pumpkin fill up that ball and we can play!

Knock knock! *Who's there?*

Cantaloupe. *Cantaloupe who?*

Cantaloupe! You're far too young!

Knock knock! *Who's there?*

Waffle. *Waffle who?*

Waffle, just waffle that I'm still standing on your step!

Knock knock! *Who's there?*

Jell-O. *Jell-O who?*

Jell-O, it's me!

8
THE "PLACE" TO BE

Knock knock! *Who's there?*

Uphill. *Uphill who?*

Uphill would make me feel better.

Knock knock! *Who's there?*

Rio. *Rio who?*

Did you Rio-range your yard ornaments?

Knock knock! *Who's there?*

Europe. *Europe who?*

Well, that's just *rude*.

Knock knock! *Who's there?*

Sicily. *Sicily who?*

Sicily question!

Knock knock! *Who's there?*

Congo. *Congo who?*

Congo to the store without your wallet!

Knock knock! *Who's there?*

Fresno. *Fresno who?*

Fresno way I'm sticking around here any longer!

Knock knock! *Who's there?*

Alaska. *Alaska who?*

Alaska 'nother house if you don't know the answer.

Knock knock! *Who's there?*

Minnesota. *Minnesota who?*

Minnesotas are fine, but I prefer extra-large ones.

Knock knock! *Who's there?*

Bucharest. *Bucharest who?*

Bucharest at the best spa!

Knock knock! *Who's there?*

Eureka. *Eureka who?*

Eureka something foul!

Knock knock! *Who's there?*

Calle. *Calle who?*

Calle-fornia is where I live.

Knock knock! *Who's there?*

Amazon. *Amazon who?*

Amazon of my mother and father.

Knock knock! *Who's there?*

Oslo. *Oslo who?*

Oslo down, what's the rush?

Knock knock! *Who's there?*

Ottawa. *Ottawa who?*

Ottawa know it's really you?

Knock knock! *Who's there?*

Samoa. *Samoa who?*

Just Samoa knock-knock jokes you haven't heard before!

Knock knock! *Who's there?*

Melbourne. *Melbourne who?*

Melbourne 13 years ago today, we have to get him a present!

Knock knock! *Who's there?*

Taipei. *Taipei who?*

Taipei 70 words a minute is really fast!

Knock knock! *Who's there?*

Toronto. *Toronto who?*

Toronto be a law against knock-knock jokes!

Knock knock! *Who's there?*

Tripoli. *Tripoli who?*

Tripoli play!

Knock knock! *Who's there?*

Cleveland. *Cleveland who?*

Cleveland and don't come back!

Knock knock! *Who's there?*

China. *China who?*

China get you to open this door is very difficult!

Knock knock! *Who's there?*

Iowa. *Iowa who?*

Iowa you one, buddy!

Knock knock! *Who's there?*

Altoona. *Altoona who?*

Altoona piano, and you can play it!

Knock knock! *Who's there?*

Eden. *Eden who?*

Eden up all your vegetables!

Knock knock! *Who's there?*

Sherwood. *Sherwood who?*

Sherwood like to come in!

Knock knock! *Who's there?*

Israel. *Israel who?*

Israel nice to meet you!

Knock knock! *Who's there?*

Peru. *Peru who?*

Peru it's really you!

Knock knock! *Who's there?*

Afghanistan. *Afghanistan who?*

Afghanistan out here all day!

Knock knock! *Who's there?*

Budapest. *Budapest who?*

You're nothing Budapest!

Knock knock! *Who's there?*

Uganda. *Uganda who?*

Uganda lot of friends when you picked up this book!

Knock knock! *Who's there?*

Quebec. *Quebec who?*

Quebec to the end of the line.

Knock knock! *Who's there?*

Marsh. *Marsh who?*

Marsh on out here!

Knock knock! *Who's there?*

Iran. *Iran who?*

Iran all the way here!

Knock knock! *Who's there?*

Havana. *Havana who?*

Havana wonderful time!

Knock knock! *Who's there?*

Kenya. *Kenya who?*

Kenya guess who this is?

Knock knock! *Who's there?*

Eiffel. *Eiffel who?*

Eiffel down, help me up!

Knock knock! *Who's there?*

Jamaica. *Jamaica who?*

Jamaica up all these jokes yourself?

Knock knock! *Who's there?*

Anthill. *Anthill who?*

Anthill-da's here again.

Knock knock! *Who's there?*

Europe. *Europe who?*

Europe to no good, I bet.

Knock knock! *Who's there?*

Ohio. *Ohio who?*

Ohio's it going?

Knock knock! *Who's there?*

Babylon. *Babylon who?*

Babylon all you want—I'm not really listening.

Knock knock! *Who's there?*

Florida. *Florida who?*

Florida bathroom is all wet!

Knock knock! *Who's there?*

B.C. *B.C. who?*

B.C.-ing you real soon, I hope.

Knock knock! *Who's there?*

Garden. *Garden who?*

Stop garden the door and let me in!

Knock knock! *Who's there?*

Aspen. *Aspen who?*

Aspen all day thinking about you!

Knock knock! *Who's there?*

Chile. *Chile who?*

It's Chile out here, open up!

Knock knock! *Who's there?*

Germany. *Germany who?*

Germany people knock on your door?

Knock knock! *Who's there?*

Uruguay. *Uruguay who?*

You go Uruguay, and I'll go mine.

Knock knock! *Who's there?*

Indonesia. *Indonesia who?*

I see you and I get weak Indonesia.

Knock knock! *Who's there?*

Russian. *Russian who?*

Stop Russian me!

Knock knock! *Who's there?*

Utah. *Utah who?*

Utah-king to me?

Knock knock! *Who's there?*

Indy. *Indy who?*

Indy upstairs bathroom!

Knock knock! *Who's there?*

York. *York who?*

York coming over to my place soon!

Knock knock! *Who's there?*

Dublin. *Dublin who?*

Dublin over in pain from laughing at all these knock-knock jokes!

Knock knock! *Who's there?*

Scotland. *Scotland who?*

Scotland on his head! Quick, call an ambulance!

Knock knock! *Who's there?*

Highway. *Highway who?*

Highway about 100 pounds.

Knock knock! *Who's there?*

Arizona. *Arizona who?*

Arizona room for one of us in this town!

Knock knock! *Who's there?*
Tunis! *Tunis who?*
Tunis company, three's a crowd!

Knock knock! *Who's there?*
Suriname. *Suriname who?*
Suriname Ariel? Because I think we *mermaid* for each other.

Knock knock! *Who's there?*
Belize. *Belize who?*
Let's fill our Belize at the buffet!

Knock knock! *Who's there?*
Rome. *Rome who?*
Rome is where the heart is!

Knock knock! *Who's there?*

France. *France who?*

France stick together, no matter what!

Knock knock! *Who's there?*

Spain. *Spain who?*

No time, I'll Spain later!

Knock knock! *Who's there?*

Detour. *Detour who?*

Detour de France comes by here in five minutes!

Knock knock! *Who's there?*

Cosmos. *Cosmos who?*

Cosmos of us are waiting outside. Let us in!

Knock knock! *Who's there?*

Armenia. *Armenia who?*

Armenia every word I say.

Knock knock! *Who's there?*

Avenue. *Avenue who?*

Avenue been missing me?

Knock knock! *Who's there?*

Aurora. *Aurora who?*

Aurora going to open the door?

Knock knock! *Who's there?*

Formosa. *Formosa who?*

Formosa the summer I stayed home.

Knock knock! *Who's there?*
Boise. *Boise who?*
Boise back in town!

Knock knock! *Who's there?*
Guinea. *Guinea who?*
Guinea five!

Knock knock! *Who's there?*
Paris. *Paris who?*
Paris good, but I'd prefer an apple.

Knock knock! *Who's there?*
Italy. *Italy who?*
Italy a shame if you don't open up!

Knock knock! *Who's there?*

Genoa. *Genoa who?*

Genoa any good places to go around here?

Knock knock! *Who's there?*

Turin. *Turin who?*

Turin to a vampire on Halloween!

Knock knock! *Who's there?*

Hallways. *Hallways who?*

Hallways knew you were mean.

Knock knock! *Who's there?*

Utica. *Utica who?*

Utica long way home, huh?

Knock knock! *Who's there?*

Tokyo. *Tokyo who?*

What Tokyo so long?

Knock knock! *Who's there?*

Heaven. *Heaven who?*

Heaven you had enough of these jokes yet?

Knock knock! *Who's there?*

Hacienda. *Hacienda who?*

Hacienda the chapter.

Knock knock! *Who's there?*
Yah. *Yah who?*
Yah who, let's party!

Knock knock! *Who's there?*
Sincerely. *Sincerely who?*
Sincerely this morning I've been waiting for you to open the door!

Knock knock! *Who's there?*

Miniature. *Miniature who?*

Miniature open your mouth, you'll say something silly!

Knock knock! *Who's there?*

Joe King. *Joe King who?*

Joe King you with another knock-knock!

Knock knock! *Who's there?*

District. *District who?*

District parents of yours means you probably can't come outside!

Knock knock! *Who's there?*

Chaos. *Chaos who?*

Chaos the letter that comes after J.

Knock knock! *Who's there?*

Riot. *Riot who?*

Riot on time!

Knock knock! *Who's there?*

Donohue. *Donohue who?*

Donohue think you can hide from me in there?

Knock knock! *Who's there?*

Duet. *Duet who?*

Duet right, or don't duet at all.

Knock knock! *Who's there?*

Hugh Cosmo. *Hugh Cosmo who?*

Hugh Cosmo trouble than anyone!

Knock knock! *Who's there?*

Oscar and Greta. *Oscar and Greta who?*

Oscar silly question . . . and Greta silly answer.

Knock knock! *Who's there?*

Carmen and Cohen. *Carmen and Cohen who?*

I can't tell if you're Carmen or Cohen.

Knock knock! *Who's there?*

Hello. *Hello who?*

My name's not who.

Knock knock! *Who's there?*

Toodle. *Toodle who?*

Toodle who to you too!

Knock knock! *Who's there?*

Gucci. *Gucci who?*

Gucci-gucci-goo!

Knock knock! *Who's there?*

Voodoo. *Voodoo who?*

Voodoo you think you are, anyway?

Knock knock! *Who's there?*

Polo. *Polo who?*

Polo-ver, you're under arrest!

Knock knock! *Who's there?*

Lotus. *Lotus who?*

Lotus in and we'll tell you.

Knock knock! *Who's there?*

Byte. *Byte who?*

Byte you're happy to see me again!

Knock knock! *Who's there?*

Amen. *Amen who?*

Amen hot water again.

Knock knock! *Who's there?*

Catch. *Catch who?*

Bless you!

Knock knock! *Who's there?*

Aldo. *Aldo who?*

Aldo anywhere with you!

Knock knock! *Who's there?*

Cain and Abel. *Cain and Abel who?*

Cain talk now . . . Abel tomorrow.

Knock knock! *Who's there?*

Datsun. *Datsun who?*

Datsun old joke.

Knock knock! *Who's there?*

Easter. *Easter who?*

Easter anybody home?

Knock knock! *Who's there?*

Myth. *Myth who?*

I myth seeing you.

Knock knock! *Who's there?*

Conrad. *Conrad who?*

Conrad-ulations, that was a great joke!

Knock knock! *Who's there?*

X. *X who?*

X me no questions, and I'll tell you no lies.

Knock knock! *Who's there?*

Yule. *Yule who?*

Yule be sorry!

Knock knock! *Who's there?*

Wendy Katz. *Wendy Katz who?*

Wendy Katz away, the mice will play!

Knock knock! *Who's there?*

Unaware. *Unaware who?*

Unaware is what you put on first!

Knock knock! *Who's there?*

Schick. *Schick who?*

Schick as a dog.

Knock knock! *Who's there?*

Sancho. *Sancho who?*

Sancho a letter, but you never replied.

Knock knock! *Who's there?*

Omega. *Omega who?*

Omega up your mind!

Knock knock! *Who's there?*

Megan, Elise, and Chicken. *Megan, Elise, and Chicken who?*

Megan, Elise, and Chicken it twice. Gonna find out who's naughty or nice . . .

Knock knock! *Who's there?*

Nana. *Nana who?*

Nana your business.

Knock knock! *Who's there?*

N.E. *N.E. who?*

N.E. body home?

Knock knock! *Who's there?*

Aloha. *Aloha who?*

Aloha myself in.

Knock knock! *Who's there?*

Flu. *Flu who?*

Hey, I wasn't crying!

Knock knock! *Who's there?*

Weird. *Weird who?*

Weird you go all day?

Knock knock! *Who's there?*

Scold. *Scold who?*

Scold out here!

Knock knock! *Who's there?*

Witch. *Witch who?*

Witch you would let me in!

Knock knock! *Who's there?*

Zombie. *Zombie who?*

The zombie who's going to break down your door!

Knock knock! *Who's there?*

Weirdo. *Weirdo who?*

Weirdo deer and the antelope play . . .

Knock knock! *Who's there?*

Waddle. *Waddle who?*

Waddle I do if you won't see me?

Knock knock! *Who's there?*

I won. *I won who?*

I won to suck your blooood!

Knock knock! *Who's there?*

Zombies. *Zombies who?*

Zombies make honey, others don't.

Knock knock! *Who's there?*

Believing. *Believing who?*

Open the door or I'll believing.

Knock knock! *Who's there?*

Disaster. *Disaster who?*

Disaster be my lucky day for once!

Knock knock! *Who's there?*

Insanity. *Insanity who?*

Don't you believe insanity Claus?

Knock knock! *Who's there?*
Says. *Says who?*
Says me, that's who!

Knock knock! *Who's there?*
Beezer. *Beezer who?*
Beezer black and yellow and live in a hive.

Knock knock! *Who's there?*
Decode. *Decode who?*
Decode is getting worse, open up!

Knock knock! *Who's there?*
Handsome. *Handsome who?*
Handsome of those cookies out here, I'm hungry!

Knock knock! *Who's there?*

Summertime. *Summertime who?*

Summertime you can be really funny, you know?

Knock knock! *Who's there?*

Oldest. *Oldest who?*

Oldest knocking is wearing me out!

Knock knock! *Who's there?*

Yellow. *Yellow who?*

Yellow! And how are you today?

Knock knock! *Who's there?*

Sizzle. *Sizzle who?*

Sizzle hurt you more than it hurts me!

Knock knock! *Who's there?*

Breed. *Breed who?*

Breed deep and say "aah!"

Knock knock! *Who's there?*

Wicked. *Wicked who?*

Wicked get dogs instead of cats, if you'd rather.

Knock knock! *Who's there?*

Value. *Value who?*

Value be my Valentine?

Knock knock! *Who's there?*

Noise. *Noise who?*

Noise to see you. How have you been?

Knock knock! *Who's there?*

Freeze. *Freeze who?*

Freeze a jolly good fellow, freeze a jolly good fellow, freeze a jolly good fellow . . . which nobody can deny!

Knock knock! *Who's there?*

Argue. *Argue who?*

Argue going to let me in?!

Knock knock! *Who's there?*

Zany. *Zany who?*

Zany-body home?

Knock knock! *Who's there?*

Justice. *Justice who?*

Justice I thought!

Knock knock! *Who's there?*

Isolate. *Isolate who?*

Isolate to the party that I almost missed it!

Knock knock! *Who's there?*

Dispense. *Dispense who?*

Dispense are too tight, I think I gained weight!

Knock knock! *Who's there?*

Jig. *Jig who?*

Jig is up! You're under arrest!

Knock knock! *Who's there?*

Vilify. *Vilify who?*

Vilify knew my name, I'd tell you!

Knock knock! *Who's there?*

Calder. *Calder who?*

Calder cops, I've been robbed!

Knock knock! *Who's there?*
July. *July who?*
July awake at night?

Knock knock! *Who's there?*
Zagat. *Zagat who?*
Zagat says "meow."

Knock knock! *Who's there?*
Bertha. *Bertha who?*
Happy Bertha Day to you . . .

Knock knock! *Who's there?*
Ashley. *Ashley who?*
Ashley's foot is making my feet all gross!

Knock knock! *Who's there?*

Fangs. *Fangs who?*

Fangs for opening the door, I'm a vampire!

Knock knock! *Who's there?*

Senior. *Senior who?*

Senior through the keyhole, so I know you're in there.

Knock knock! *Who's there?*

Lucretia. *Lucretia who?*

Lucretia from the Black Lagoon!

Knock knock! *Who's there?*

Eyes darted. *Eyes darted who?*

Eyes darted to droop but I woke up!

Knock knock! *Who's there?*

Itch. *Itch who?*

Itch a long time coming!

Knock knock! *Who's there?*

Censor. *Censor who?*

Censor so smart, you tell me!

Knock knock! *Who's there?*

Vampire. *Vampire who?*

Vampire State Building!

Knock knock! *Who's there?*

Blue. *Blue who?*

Blue your nose on your sleeve again, huh?

10
SO RANDOM!

Knock knock! *Who's there?*
To. *To who?*
It's "To whom?"

Knock knock! *Who's there?*
Event. *Event who?*
Event that-a-way!

Knock knock!

Who's there?

D-1.

D-1 who?

D-1 who knocked!

Knock knock!

Who's there?

Kimberly.

Oh, hi, Kimberly come in, come in!

No! You're supposed to say "Kimberly who?"!

Knock knock!

Who's there?

I don't know.

I don't know who?

I don't know who either,
so open up and find out!

Knock knock!

Who's there?

Atom.

Atom who?

Atom up, $5 + 5 = 10$.

Knock knock!

Who's there?

Amnesia.

Amnesia who?

Oh, you have it too?

Knock knock!

Who's there?

Ben and Don.

Ben and Don who?

Ben there. Don that.

Knock knock!

Who's there?

Easily distracted zombie.

Easily distracted zombie who?

Hey, look, a chicken!

You ever wonder why there aren't any knock-knock jokes about America?

Because freedom rings!

Knock knock! *Who's there?*

Knock knock! *Knock knock who?*

Knock knock! *Who's there?*

Knock knock! *Knock knock who?*

Knock knock! *Who's there?*

Knock knock! *Knock knock who?*

Knock knock! *Who's there?*

Orange. *Orange who?*

Orange you glad I didn't say "Knock knock"?

Knock knock! *Who's there?*

Electra. *Electra who?*

Electricity! Isn't that shocking?

Knock knock! *Who's there?*

Will you remember me in an hour? *Yes.*

In a day? *Yes.*

In a week? *Yes.*

In a month? *Yes.*

In a year? *Yes.*

I think you won't. *Yes, I will.*

Knock knock! *Who's there?*

You've forgotten *already?!*

Why did the chicken cross the road? *Why?*

To get to your house.

Knock knock! *Who's there?*

The chicken!

Knock knock!

Who's there?

Dandelion.

Dandelion who?

Dandelion is a very fancy lion!

Knock knock!

Who's there?

Fink.

Fink who?

Fink you can stand to hear another knock-knock joke?

Knock knock!

Who's there?

It's me, your good friend.

Oh, please come in, what a nice surprise!

Knock knock!

Who's there?

Spell.

Spell who?

Okay, W-H-O.

Knock knock! *Who's there?*

Jim Billy Bob Jones, Jr. *Jim Billy Bob Jones, Jr. who?*

Seriously? How many guys named Jim Billy Bob Jones, Jr. do you know?

Knock knock! *Who's there?*

Time traveler. *Time traveler who?*

See you yesterday!

Knock knock! *Who's there?*

4. *4 who?*

4 whom the bell tolls! *But you knocked.*

Oh yeah!

Knock knock! *Who's there?*

A magically refilling glass of soda.

Well, come on in!

Knock knock! *Who's there?*

Yumara. *Yumara who?*

Will Yumara me?

Knock knock! *Who's there?*

Adam's not. *Adam's not who?*

Adam's not is dripping from Adam's nose.

Knock knock!

Who's there?

Gas.

Gas who?

It's me!

Knock knock!

Who's there?

Grr.

Grr who?

So, are you a bear or an owl?

Knock knock!

Who's there?

Hi.

Hi who?

Hi object to this line of questioning!

Knock knock!

Who's there?

Veer.

Veer who?

Veer verr you on the night of the 20th?

Knock knock!

Who's there?

Emily.

Emily who?

I have no idea. My name is Dave.

Knock knock!

Who's there?

Area.

Area who?

Area there? It's me!

Knock knock!

Come on in, it's open.

Knock knock! *Who's there?*

I am. *I am who?*

You mean you don't remember who you are?

Knock knock! *Who's there?*

You know, *You know who?*

Oh no, it's You-know-who!

Knock knock!

Who's there?

Knock knock!

Who's there?

No, you're supposed to say, "Knock knock who?"!

Knock knock!

Who's there?

Impatient pirate.

Impatient pirate wh—

Arrrr!

Knock knock!

Who's there?

Opportunity.

Opportunity who?

Hey, opportunity doesn't knock twice!

Knock knock!

Who's there?

Howdy.

Howdy who?

No, not howdy who, howdy do!

Knock knock!

Who's there?

Armageddon.

Armageddon who?

Armageddon a new friend!

Knock knock!

Who's there?

Wah.

Wah who?

Well, why are *you* so happy, huh?

Knock knock!

Who's there?

Some.

Some who?

Some goofball telling you a knock-knock joke.

Did you hear about the person who invented the knock-knock joke?

They were just awarded the No-Bell Prize!

Knock knock!

Who's there?

You're not.

You're not who?

You're not the smartest person, are you?

Knock knock!

Who's there?

[fill in your own name]

[name] who?

[name]! Don't you recognize my voice? It's me, your own child!